Rays

RICHARD PRICE was born in 1966 and grew up in Scotland. His previous collections include *Lucky Day* (2005), which focuses on the world of his daughter Katie, who has Angelman's Syndrome, and *Greenfields* (2007), a collection of poems about childhood, family, and memory. *Lucky Day* was a Book of the Year in *The Guardian* and in *Scotland on Sunday*, and was shortlisted for several prizes, including the Whitbread. *Greenfields* was shortlisted for the Sundial Scottish Arts Council Poetry Book of the Year. His poems have been translated into French, Finnish, German, Hungarian and Portuguese. He has also published short stories and literary criticism, and has collaborated in the creation of artists' books and installations. Richard Price is Head of Modern British Collections at the British Library, London.

D1461831

RICHARD PRICE

Rays

CARCANET

First published in Great Britain in 2009 by
Carcanet Press Limited
Alliance House
Cross Street
Manchester M2 7AQ

A CIP catalogue record for this book is available from the British Library
ISBN 978 84777 010 3

The publisher acknowledges financial assistance from Arts Council England

Supported by
ARTS COUNCIL
ENGLAND

Typeset by XL Publishing Services, Tiverton
Printed and bound in England by SRP Ltd, Exeter

for B

Acknowledgements

Some of the poems in this collection first appeared in the following limited editions *Earliest Spring Yet* (Landfill Press), *Lute Variations* (Rack Press), and *little but often* (with Ronald King, Circle Press). Some have appeared in *Atlas*, *Booklight* (Knucker Press), *fragmente*, *Markings*, *PN Review*, *Poetry International*, *R.U. Taking the Biscuit?* (University of Reading), *The Thing That Mattered Most* (Scottish Poetry Library), and *The Times Literary Supplement*: my thanks to all the editors involved.

'Wake Up and Sleep' was commissioned by Lavinia Greenlaw in a project by the Calouste Gulbenkian Foundation in association with the Royal Society of Medicine, and a version was first published in *Signs and Rumours* published by the Foundation. My thanks to Dr Peter Venn for discussing his work on the treatment of sleep disorders. *Wake Up and Sleep* was later developed as a limited edition artists' book in collaboration with the artist Caroline Isgar.

A number of the 'Songs for the Loss Adjusters' have been set to music by Caroline Trettine and recorded by Mirabeau.

Dorothy Stirling's *Passing Acquaintance* was painted specifically for this collection and is reproduced here with kind permission – and in admiration.

My thanks, too, to David K. for reading and commenting on the manuscript of this book.

Contents

Freehold

A summer's day? – you're
lovelier... You're... more gentle.

Gales shake May's sweetheart buds,
summer holds a short-term lease –
one minute the sun is foundry hot,
the next all gold is lost.

The season's fairs, too, so easily decline – bad luck reigns,
rivers reclaim their rightful plain.

But your summer won't dim, won't flood,
you won't lose, love, the celebration
your self-contained self, almost by itself, contains.
Death won't claim you mooch in his twenty-four-hour mall.
That boast is nearer mine –
in these eternal lines you walk right by my side.

So long as folk can breathe or eyes can see
so this will live, and this gives life to you and me.

William Shakespeare (trans.)

Wake Up and Sleep

The thought keeps counting

The weight of my own eyes.
I have a forehead. A mouth,
dry. The thought –

the thought   the thought   the thought

★

Overheated. A wash of the face
and it's right cold if you run the tap.

★

A drink of the old polar covalent,
ache too oh. Simple. Can work.

★

Not this time.

★

the thought   the thought   the thought

★

Drowsy in charge of a photocopier.

'Off coffee, thanks.'

The tea's buzzless, camomile and calm.
I'm gulping watercolours, columnists' remedies.

★

the thought

★

The thought keeps counting. Can the thought
just stop counting?

★

Lives in the linear programming, people in the detail.

★

the thought   the thought

★

Drowsy in charge of a people carrier.

★

The night's *A–Z* is stuck at Why.
Anyone know Zed Street?

'In your dreams.'

★

With primary insomnia the data suggests
there's *decreased* regional cerebral blood flow (rCBF)
to the frontal medial, occipital and parietal cortices,
and to the basal ganglia. I'll explain these things later.
Countries of the brain. Decrease, yes. Surprising
when you don't think about it.

We know behavioural therapy for insomnia (BT-I) works
but how does it work? Definitive conclusions
are just not possible but first indications –
it's just one study – but first indications
suggest successful treatment is associated
(I have to emphasise it's an association at this point),
with a *reversal* in cerebral deactivation.

★

the thought   the thought   the thought

★

The thought was only thinking,
the thought just doesn't think.

You just don't think, do you?

★

Subjects were diagnosed through interviews,
psychometrics, blood chemistries, sleep diaries.

Patients underwent three nights of polysomnographic testing
and on Night 3, ten minutes after the first K-complex / sleep spindle
they were infused with 25mCi of Tc-99m-HMPAO.

Sorry, yes, infused means injected.

Twelve minutes after injection we wakened the subjects.
They were scanned.

On diary measures all patients exhibited improvements in sleep
(including, in layman's terms, falling to sleep quicker;
night wakenings fewer).

The SPECT results you know:
while it appears that insomnia may be experienced by the sufferer
as thinking too much – the behaviour of 'a worrier'
or, temporarily, a victim of inspiration –
objective analysis associates this variety of sleeplessness
with reduced cerebral activity.

A healthy sleeper has a lively sleeping mind?

★

Behavioural therapy does tend to work
but unlearning the anxiety of the bedroom is seen as 'not medical'.
It is certainly expensive. Funding sessions with a sleep therapist
would give the Health Service sleepless nights. Huh!

Zed drugs are cheap to make, cheap to administer.
They are effective, for as long as they are taken. Then:
to break the pattern.

But in sleep, Zed is the last word.

★

The last word?

Sleep, be your kindness.
Kindle slumber now. Let tenderness and balm be your touching
                                                    flames.
Consume unthinking thought. Welcome me this anxious night
with gentle oblivion.

★

Drowsy in charge of

Drowsy in charge of

Drowsy in charge of
a king-sized kingdom of good nights.

'Night.'

Continuous Positive Air Pressure

My age your muscles are under more strain. They're in the neck, like guy ropes. Yes I like a sandwich, a lemon shandy. (Snoresville, but I didn't know it.) 'Please, wake up and pipe down.' My clothes are tentish, too, 'My buffalo pavilion.'

Obstructive apnoea: long-suffering partners hawsering their long-haul snufflers in. The livids and the oblivious.

The endurance of affection is a marriage, all kinds of sleeplessness and it is a killer. A classic motorway accident – waking in the swerve – or a door banging across the hours, not quite each, not quite every.

Tonight I settle with a mask on my face, captain of the jet, and the compressor gives you breath, a mask on my face waiting (we're both loaded with waiting – 'Remember, the bedroom is not a fearful place.'). We're waiting for the flight, to be unthinking. We're waiting for the benevolent stratosphere of nothing. From first officer to last passenger we crave a currency measured in dreams, to be torpor millionaires. We're waiting to cross goodnight's tender continent, goodnight's tender continent. Cross, we're waiting – to cross. Cross the. To cross goodnight. To cross.

Out-for-the-Count.

Wake up and sleep

Drowsy finalising the blueprint,
drowsy verifying the footprint.
Drowsy in data entry,
drowsy on checkpoint sentry,
drowsy and missing the asset-stripping on Dead Street.

Half-asleep, fingertipping the spreadsheet,
thumbing the defective directory
of on-the-mind on-the-mend half-attended ex's.
Half-asleep and just holding on
to the handholds in the homemade purgatory
of six-of-one custody fro-and-to vexes.
Half asleep quoting chapter and hexes
from the ratified sleepwalking directive.

Wake up outside your conscientious waking dream,
wake up and sleep.
Wake up outside your ache, your late luscious just-what-it-seems,
wake up and sleep.
Wake up to the what-happened, wake up to the casehardened,
wake up between look and leap.
Wake up in the shatter and decade-seep,
wake up and sleep.

Say goodnight to shaking –
there's a wake in over-waking.
Scowls and scarlatina are the stories in the clinic cantina:
more at the morgue does tend to mean less.
Owls and the ocarina are glories in the night arena
but leave them for a week, I guess.
(Sleep's demeanour improves life's fever –
you need to nod to get to yes.)

Peace and quiet for the codes and the kids,
for the didn't-halfs and the nearly-dids. Rest your roads, your
well-rids.
Peace and quiet for the sky-deep, ocean-high equation.
No tended-baggage advantage-adage panic profiticians. No
palpitations.
Peace and quiet for the offence-taking nations-within-nations.
Peace. Not a peep. Please,
sleep.

Lute Variations

Improvisations after Louise Labé

Your eyes translate me

Ô beaux yeux bruns, ô regards détournés,
Ô chauds soupirs, ô larmes épandues,
Ô noires nuits vainement attendues,
Ô jours luisants vainement retournés!

Ô tristes plaints, ô désirs obstinés,
Ô temps perdu, ô peines dépendues,
Ô milles morts en mille rets tendues,
Ô pires maux contre moi destinés!

Ô ris, ô front, cheveux, bras, mains et doigts!
Ô luth plaintif, viole, archet et voix!
Tant de flambeaux pour ardre une femelle!

De toi me plains, que tant de feux portant,
En tant d'endroits d'iceux mon coeur tâtant,
N'en est sur toi volé quelque étincelle.

Louise Labé

Your eyes translate me. You look – look away.
Sighs. Close to tears. Crush. 'The first sign of rain.'
The night is my master, in thrall in vain.
Dawn breaks? Lush nothing again, just the day.

A sob saga, this obstinate desire.
Count the ache on ache. Count the months elapsed!
Count a thousand deaths in a thousand traps,
bad luck stacked up, right perfect for a pyre.

It's smile and ear – forehead, hair – hands, fingers!
It's plaintive lute, voice, song – loss that lingers! –
so many flames when just one match would do!

What hurts most, when you wield your blazing brand,
when you cauterise my heart's wound: you stand
outside the heat. Not a spark touches you.

★

15

Eyes... turned away.
Warm rain.
What to say.
Dawn... dawns. Nothing again.

Full obstinate desire.
Ache on ache. Months elapsed.
'A thousand deaths, a thousand traps.'
Stack the pyre.

Your fingers! Your smile!
Your song the homeward mile.
The flames you command
when just one match would do!

And when your blazing brand
welds shut this heart, not a spark touches you.

★

eyes away
rain
say
nothing again

obstinate desire
months elapsed
deaths traps
stack the pyre

smile
the homeward mile
you command
just do

blazing brand
this you

From the moment

Tout aussitôt que je commence à prendre
Dans le mol lit le repos désiré,
Mon triste esprit, hors de moi retiré,
S'en va vers toi incontinent se rendre.

Lors m'est avis que dedans mon sein tendre
Je tiens le bien où j'ai tant aspiré,
Et pour lequel j'ai si haut soupiré
Que de sanglots ai souvent cuidé fendre.

O doux sommeil, ô nuit à moi heureuse!
Plaisant repos plein de tanquillité,
Continuez toutes les nuits mon songe;

Et si jamais ma pauvre âme amoureuse
Ne doit avoir de bien en vérité,
Faites au moins qu'elle en ait en mensonge.

Louise Labé

From the moment I welcome to my bed
long pursued, long desired sleep,
my creature thought starts its creep,
crawls, no, runs, flies to you instead.

Then I'm gripped, or held, or fed
by everything I've hoped for, hold deep.
Agonised sighs seem trite, pat, cheap.
I soon forget what idle anguish said.

Sweet sleep. A night, perhaps, of happiness.
Sultry slumber, the tease of tranquility –
lavish, please, all my nights with such slow dreams

and if it's no to love, to tenderness,
no to the sweetest in all humanity,
let me at least enjoy the feast – of all that seems.

★

From the minute I welcome to my bed
long pursued, long desired sleep,
my creature thought starts its creep –
steps – no, sprints – flies to you instead.

The flickers continue within this head:
I hold the prize I've longed for,
the one I've sighed, sobbed and wronged for,
the one who left me close to dead.

Sweet sleep. A night, perhaps, of happiness,
sultry slumber's tease. Tranquility,
allow me, please, these luxuriant dreams.

And if it's no to love, to tenderness,
no to that dear distant reality,
let me embrace sleep's soft grace: all that seems.

★

from my bed
pursued desired sleep
creature creep
to you instead

flickers head
prize longed for
sighed wronged for
close to dead

perhaps happiness
tranquility
please dreams

no tenderness
no reality
all that seems

Lute, companion

Luth, compagnon de ma calamité,
De mes soupirs témoin irréprochable,
De mes ennuis contrôleur véritable,
Tu as souvent avec moi lamenté

Et tant le pleur piteux t'a molesté
Que, commençant quelque son délectable,
Tu le rendais tout soudain lamentable,
Feignant le ton que plein avais chanté.

Et si tu veux efforcer au contraire,
Tu te détends et si me contrains taire:
Mais me voyant tendrement soupirer,

Donnant faveur à ma tant triste plainte,
En mes ennuis me plaire suis contrainte
Et d'un doux mal douce fin espérer.

Louise Labé

Lute, companion in this catastrophe movie,
witness to each and every tear,
I was down, drugged, dragged distant –
you brought me near.
Master, you endured disaster, just to soothe me.

My sobs haven't only upset you:
I start a song, picking joy,
a simple tale, a girl, a boy,
you end it badly. I let you.

But when I insist, play rough, act mean,
you resist, silence sound and shut up scene.
Only whispers, sung tear by tear,

revive your care, de-scorch the torch song.
Your tone is warming right, not burn-down wrong.
Old friend all along, you're heart, hope, sincere.

Lute, you're here.

★

Lute, friend in this disaster,
witness to these tears,
mentor, maid, fond master,
father before these fears,

sob on sob has upset you
transforming delighting tones.
Rich harmonies I let you
degrade to keens, to moans.

I... imposed, and grief's recklessness
finally made you mute.
Only thought in tenderness
revived my beloved lute.

All my cares, concerns, you were at last pleased to calm.
From thought's sorrow, the lull, the balm.

★

lute disaster
witness tears
mentor master
father fears

sob upset you
delighting tones
rich I let you
degrade moans

imposed recklessness
finally mute
thought tenderness
revived lute

cares calm
lull balm

Earliest Spring Yet

About this

An intrusion? – to think of you

walking and thinking, walking and

not thinking – of me –
I guess.

I...
hope not

(an intrusion,
not not thinking...

of...).

A 'double positive'? –
thinking thinking? Thinking thinking

this way?

The idea

I know I can't mean
as much to you
as you me. I

don't know. Your
meaning, your
meaning. Nothing

is secure, the idea.
Boundlessness.
Short of breath.

I know there's who
and there's… the idea,
the idea of who. I

don't know. 'I
don't-feel-the-same-way' –
but you

trust me – entrust
confidences –
are right to.

A friendship of months
yet I kiss
as a friend,

almost a friend,
of years. I…
'try-to-keep-things-light'

and I hope.

Manet with Mardy

We laughed
at a masterpiece.
The subject
became the word.

I saw
pride at least –
(strength, strength
in the absurd) –

met
the glance's claim...
'Love times laughs!'
'Full light!'

'Mardy',
my name...
for 'Mardy',
not here tonight.

Formal

Waking without you.

I love you like sleep.
Left the radio on, dance
coming down.

A formal kiss –
everyone touches

more these days –

that formal first kiss.
Yesterday today.

The last?

Melancholy plumber

She's got a
> *melancholy <u>plumber</u>,*
fixes all her
> *taps and pipes.*
She's got a
> *<u>melancholy</u> plumber,*
fixes all her
> *taps and pipes.*
I could be her
> *<u>happy-go-lucky</u> plumber*
fix things just the way she likes.

I'm in trouble,
in trouble with me and you.
I'm in trouble,
in trouble
> with me and you.
Said I thought a bit about you.
That statement was economic with the truth.

She's got a
> *melancholy <u>plumber</u>,*
fixes all her
> *taps and pipes.*
She's got a
> *<u>melancholy</u> plumber,*
fixes <u>all</u> her
> *taps and pipes.*
I could be her
> *<u>happy-go-lucky</u> plumber*
fix things <u>just</u> the way she likes.

I'm in trouble,
in trouble with me and <u>you</u>.
I'm in trouble,
trouble with me and <u>you</u>.
Said I thought a lot about you.
That statement
was economic with the truth.

She's got a
　　　　melancholy plumber,
fixes all her taps and pipes.
She's got a
　　　　melancholy plumber,
fixes all her taps and pipes.
I could be her
　　　　happy-go-lucky plumber
fix things just the way she likes.

A shape, the past

Love *was* –
a shape, the past,

a... structure.

In love – 'in'
'is'.

I, I... I?

you/her   I
her/you   I

tell me   tell me   tell me
tell me   tell me   tell me

Don't tell me.

Off, on

I hope detective shows solve something.
Process and forensics, trusty as a good sheen.

You have to believe in accumulated law,
and handguns? Handguns –

weapons of mass flickering captions…
Is that right?

Calm yourself (yourself).
One machine off, on the other.

A song –
words not fine, tune not fine.

Fine.

As if a song

She sends me sensual records –
I know she's not leading me on.
I started the lending library,
books and poems, off and on.
    I've loved her since
    I saw the hints
    of the planet I was living on,
    her planet.

Sharing songs is intimate –
it's hearing singing in the shower?
It's voice and face,
it's lips and poise – and power.
    I hear her songs
    and sing along.
    I sing badly, but I bless the hour,
    I bless this planet.

She's half reluctant,
I hope she's not being kind.
She knows I'm trouble,
trouble I can't leave behind.
    I'm afraid
    one fine day
    she'll leave *me* behind,
        silent blue planet.

Babyshambles

A dim view of the fighting, who
strutted it? Pete come on
act your get-together.

Stage empty and full-lit, no
here he's back and the band
all friends, at odds for the re-kick.

A couple of hump-shunted songs,
exit.

Resonant frequency

Records, some books,
my resonant frequency:
I'm not quite here
and twice the size.

Chatter, then a few words
direct to camera. Oh I like him, I like her,
informal today.
I'm almost in their company –
one direction,
except the licence.

Books, frequency, here.
Sighs – words – her.
Today, company direction, licence.

Hear her licence.

Channel Link

Even stations move.

Can I meet you fifteen years ago
by the sprung chainlink?

We could watch together those ever-afters
waiting for a platform. The go-ahead
and they're polite about it.

Sandstone dust, and not now the long settled past –
construction grit in a suspension of air.

I could meet you fifteen minutes ago
at the same coordinates.
I'm watch-wiping on the interim platform.

For once I'm not about
to be all that late,
give or take, and if you'd show up
not even half apologising (not that you –)
between yesterday and now, or simply tomorrow
I'd class that on time.

A century find

High up the beach, sea debris resolved in lines –
brittle black – dry seaweed and ribboned bark. That's

a stretching step.
We've gained the sand.

Footfall hallmarks the sifted acres.
We're goldsmiths of the shifting commonwealth,
brand in bulk.

Outpace the gusts and there's a rock to race to,
exceed. The tide

is lapping away (the force in gentleness):
we're the centre of all murmur –
no ocean can shoosh us.

Slowly, secrets. The confidence to confide…
I was, you were… I am, you are…

★

In your displaying hand a hard small shell,
offwhite, convincing pure,
drilled the once with a dainty calibre
(incremental parasite or shock-quick beak?)

Hard? – frail, sea-crushable.
Creature-perfected, capable
of a low whistle. Strung on silver,
the central jewel: a century find
to fulfil a necklace.

You throw it – so far out
it's still in your fist.

Volume

Back to the rock, lured
by pools in the lee.

Startled sea anemones trust at last
the volume of stillness, open.

Shells

Ache to know –
or just hold.

How much
is there?

It's what you think.

Shells mock the ear.
Shallows? The swell?

New / Just healed. Howls
mock the air. Howls
mock the scar.

Look – that was you,
I think.

Internationalist

'You can sleep for England' –
and Scotland, too.

I come round
inside my skin –
and fill myself with you.

Earliest spring yet

Heavy as humming birds
nearly-clumsy bumble bees
busy themselves
in the white-and-pink.

How do you
praise, and seek
not to shake the complexity?

A tense cherry tree
in fullest blossom, surprised
at its own beauty, caught
in its as-ifs.

'Earliest spring yet –
I hope
it hasn't tricked them.'

Flax

There are two kinds of flax – the first
has blue flowers.

I picked some this morning,
oversleeping

in a shimmering Lincolnshire field.

Simple clothing and sheets –
they keep temperatures low.

The other flax
is a bluer blue this time
(my reference books don't have enough pictures).

I picked some this morning,
trekking back from that radiant Lincolnshire.

This flax endures, bluesy at the roadside.
It cheers a place up, kept to a small vase.

(Varnish – a layer
to seal this spoken
painting, your painting.)

Shades on

Slowed and I
caught up with the close-up, you

know how to share a smile –

between you and you
and me –

lucky as a don't-deserve-it –
that's the definition of luck –

'that's the definition
of anything'

Yes I do believe
(strong sunshine)

there is a need –

grey-green blue eyes
have to look out.

Wren

A tidy wren, tiny apron on,
spot-checks the garden.

Not a speck —
she's gone.

Age of Exploration

island that tides keep sipping

song of restless travelling

waves of gentle lapping

a wakening a caressing

find of a life's ocean

a seeking soft resolving

tremors of the shoreline

we're us, we're you and I

near transparent morning

moments and glisten

your whispering your shimmer

improving the silence

your room a garden

dew of a dream's waiting

rays that now curve you

our us and you and I

all the allness for a second –

thought and its translation

music of longing

landfall yet cloister

between bud and flowering

intimate suspension

a shyness of singing

we are us and you and I

The long low structure

the long low structure

the water-meadow an outpost the outpost 'choose
the new international'

chevrons, and planes are chevrons

on the concrete, stairs on wheels, single-purpose vehicles

offwhites and greys, silvers that will not glint

        a change –
        of muscle density, the face –
        tense – the face was tense, 'not exactly
        worried', good
        to see you

        'and you'

Dippers –

stout black-and-white birds
the guarded river stewards

(the word stalwart
the word boulder)

the glisten of decelerating shallows

rocks
and bright green riverweed

the banks are broken
but it's not a catastrophe

young lithe trees
with their socks wet

underwater 'chubsters' –
the unhurried dippers

try that, skinnymalinks

Languor's Whispers

Straps stripped,
tans' stripes,
laps and lips, lush
soft locks.

Languor's whispers
to longing, listening.

★

The release

of play and please,
quietly now allowed.

Two
perfects the crowd.

★

A lick, a life.
The lyric lazed within,
the link

of glow and glimpse,
the jewels
of just ourselves.

★

Lying in.

Lambency from shirk,
the glints
from whys and whines
(work), the shoosh
of sigh-by-sigh
drumming of the hum.

★

Friendless.

Hand-in-hand's routine
routed, de-planned:
forwarder, franker, fresher,
serious leisure.

Louts – us –
dedicated layabouts,
blunt
and blameless (would-be).

★

Touch, and touch's could-be
deep shallows, lap
and kiss, sense-sipping lips,
finger-tips.

★

The taste-sniff
sniff-taste
hear of here,
the see

of near-bounded, no,
the near-boundless sea.

★

Touch, touch, touch.

Hopes, love, luck,
perfect just,
a right too much.

Songs for the Loss Adjusters

Parkway

Is this the North?
Rain pavements, salt severe?
Canal to Canada,
hard freight beer?

I've been hereabouts
just passing through.
Stopped at the Parkway –
didn't see you.

The West's attractive,
mermaids in nets.
Credit card pagans,
crabster bets.

I've been nearly there,
time off in lieu.
Stopped at the Parkway
waiting for you.

The Parkway, the promise. The Parkway
one more transfer on.
I saw you once – pleading on the platform,
last train gone.

Suffolk for Saxons,
mudflats, ice-cream.
Kings in the crakefields,
vicars by the team.

I've been close, or close enough,
an hour or two.
I stopped at the Parkway,
nothing to do.

Sample the South
for giants, horses, fire.
Cliffs retreat before bare feet,
cathedrals cage the choir.

Thanks for the tip,
that's one I'll pursue.
Meet me at the Parkway,
late will do.

Work's over

Eyesmile, lipsmile,
a public secret peck on the cheek.
Your style is my style –
love, if you believe it, love at its peak.

Work's over and I
haven't been waiting,
I haven't been waiting,
I haven't been waiting for long.

Overthrow the system
or just fine-tune?
Draft or bottled?
Double gins this late afternoon?

Take them down with you?
Toe the line?
A letter to a paper?
Just resign?

Work's over and I
haven't been waiting,
I haven't been waiting,
I haven't been waiting for long.

You're thinking aloud, a sparkling power –
your seconds ignite the hour.
You're back on earth, back to you.
Laughter, ideas, the real work we do.

Company, euphoria – that's my task.
You can join in, you know – you don't have to ask.

Work's over and I
haven't been waiting,
I haven't been waiting,
I haven't been waiting for long.

Hometime, alonetime,
the shortest walk, a brief goodbye.
Separation's simple –
it's you and yours, it's me myself I.

(Eyesmile, lipsmile,
a public secret peck on the cheek.
Your style is my style –
love, if you believe it, love at its peak.)

I believe it, I believe it, I
believe.

Trackside fires

Trackside fires when we met,
foxes confused.
Dust and drought, reservoir regret,
underloved and overused.

'Quench,' you said –
least, that's what I thought I heard.
States get complicated
scorched up in a word.

'There could be water,
rescue without cease.
Take it from a loss adjuster,
take it from a fireman's niece.'

Trackside fires when we met,
foxes confused.
Dust and drought, reservoir regret,
underloved and overused.

Meadow plots, a gated tranche,
one to seventy.
'No hidden costs', exclusive lots,
one-offs a-plenty.

I'm half-asleep –
I'm in the age of steam.
I stagger up for my station stop,
I walk right out the dream.

Trackside fires when we met,
foxes confused.
Dust and drought, reservoir regret,
underloved, overused.

These days I'm temperamental –
I gulp down Now, I sweat out the past.
And I hear you're wise, or sly, or sentimental,
I hear you've claimed peace at last.

I don't regret regrets,
I'm just sorry for the thirst.
What a drinker soon forgets
family pick up cursed...

Trackside fires when we met,
foxes confused.
Dust and drought, reservoir regret,
underloved, overused.

Ambulance work

Give up the ambulance work –
I know you're specialised
in the drunk and justified,
in geniuses
of bad luck and spite –
oh the cream, the cream
of Saturday night.
I know you're a heart-start engineer.
But give up the ambulance work –
drive back here.

Your latest case paged your purse
while your highness did slumber.
Why'd you give him your withheld number?
I told him
please remember
if it's not what you mean, grief's obscene,
go call your mother,
go volunteer.
Give up the ambulance work –
fling yourself clear.

A friend, they said, called as well –
I felt I had to answer.
Was it Jerry or Sammy or Charlie-Ray Chancer?
You'd know,
my lavish life-enhancer
by his tone of wheedle and scream –
by his threat of curse and cancer
if you didn't dance the Magic Reappear.
Give up the deliverance work,
stop right here.

You're a caring person –
that's what all the surveys say.
Yes, you drive too fast,
misapply the Elastoplast,
you can lose your urgent way.
There are complications you can't foresee –
there can't always be a happy survival
for each and every A&E arrival
you hold close, you hold dear.
Give up the clairvoyance work –
your future's here.

I can't persuade you – I see that now.
I've known it all along.
You're above weak or strong,
anaesthetised
from right or wrong,
above advice, I mean,
a healing song.
You're above waiting to hear.
Stick with the ambulance work –
it's a glittering career.

Two halves of nothing

If 'Two halves of nothing'
cuts out on the radio,
if the river's up
past the stereo,
if everything good
you needed to know
gets lost in the flood,
you remember it
after love.

Remember the bridge,
remember the edge,
remember
remembering a kiss?

Remember
we should know better,
better than this:
'Two halves of nothing'
doesn't exist.

If your ex wants something
you can't see through,
if they ask what's what
or you say 'I do',
if none of us could
be all that true,
courtesy bad blood,
you remember it
after love.

Remember the bridge,
remember the edge,
remember
remembering a kiss?

Remember
we should know better,
better than this:
'Two halves of nothing'
doesn't exist.

Last train, full of couples

Last train, full of couples.
I shouldn't have shouted.
Last train, full of couples.
You took drugs in the Listening Olympics.
Last train, full of couples.
There are worse things than an honest debate.
No goodbye this time?
Last train, full of couples.
All stations
to the end of the line.

Last train, full of couples.
You'll be home I guess.
Last train, full of couples.
These two aren't speaking but she's staying close.
Last train, full of couples.
Alright we disagree – on faith and the shimmering law.
Is that a High Court crime?
Last train, full of couples.
All stations
to the end of the line.

Last train full of couples.
You'll still be awake.
Last train, full of couples.
Red bra straps and a silver stud.
Last train, full of couples.
Roman earrings, stolen within a week.
Minerva, in her prime.
Last train, full of couples.
All stations
to the end of the line.

Last train, first train – midnight's delivered
its prizewinning song.
The passengers are passionate,
they're clutching and clinging.
The ticket collector's singing
'Let's Get It On'.

Last train, full of couples.
Your eyes – surely closed by now.
Last train, full of couples.
You always sleep with conviction.
Last train, full of couples.
Tattoos on my shoulder, a birthmark on your thigh –
everything's flames to me.
Last train, full of couples.
Kids and pensioners travel free.

I'm writing to write again

I'm writing to write again
and you

also, as well as, too?

I'm phoning to phone again
and you –

also, as well as, too?

'Memories are melodies' –
they charm the pulse
        to a residue.
Shall I hum one
        now I'm here?
You don't disappear
        for an hour or two

also, as well as, too.

We'll not disappear
for a day or two,

also, as well as, too.

We're singing,
just me, just you,

also, as well as, too.

[Hidden track]

I won the lottery
but my ticket got lost in the wash.
   Spin, spin, washing machine.
   Spin, spin, wheel of fortune.

We'd agreed to cease to cheat –
you burst in round about then.
You put two and two together,
and multiplied by ten.

Oh, I won the lottery
but my ticket got lost in the wash.
   Spin, spin, washing machine.
   Spin, spin, wheel of fortune.

You were my prize, my fill-your-trolley,
my river apartment keys.
All bets are off, I'm null and void.
No publicity, please.

Oh, I won the lottery
but my ticket got lost in the wash.
   Spin, spin, washing machine.
   Spin, spin, wheel of fortune.

little but often

a

absolute beginner,
a little shy

asked directions –
so did I

b

blame the books, blame the bees

blame the feathered creatures, the boyish features,
the emblem on the tree –

blame me

c

course you can,
daily and late at night –

any time and many the time
is perfectly alright

d

dare I
dare I
dare –

dreams demand distance

e

everything you said I hear
concentrated in a phrase

I'm a paid-up human summariser
these days

f

fever – call it that –
you wouldn't be the first

it's fire, my friend,
fire and fear and thirst

g

ghosts of lovers thrive –

I'm the howling spirit,
they're the ones alive

*(gravity-fugitive,
sight's sift –*

*hard g, soft g,
light's silent gift)*

h

hesitations

share a life –
halve it?

i

spark / ember / fire

ifs focus anguish,
hopes elaborate desire

j

snack wrappers and receipts
clog the gardens by the cars

jonquils –
their quiet citrus stars

k

lips to lips,
lips on supersensitive skin

a kiss is a conclusive start –
where do I begin?

1

lavish love

m

more of musk, more of mess,
more is a must –

may I suggest we both invest
in a high frisk mutual trust?

n

nobody and never,
not forgetting now –

categorical ballads
freeze and scorch somehow

o

only you said

only
said you

only us

p

perfect
or approximately ideal –
perfect

(real)

q

quested for you –
ultimate, intimate prize –

is it so wrong to lust and long?
my saint, is it wise?

r

not play-acting – rough

you've been hurt before?

tough

S

I saved your texts
and they saved me

say nothing now
or yes / well… / we'll see

t

temptiness

u

advice on until,
advice on unless –

finish with ultimatums,
begin with finesse

V

violets –

a second's
intense scent...

numbness

w

weight of why,
weight of when –

answer by mirror /
barcode pen

X

just an extra –
no speaking part

pre-loved –
exchange and mart

(exhale, detox, unflex –
let the hex do the max – relax –
no one's just an ex)

y

try or toy?
yes, say, or yet?

years and rays

your eyes

z

not zero – angry silence
not zero – self-righteous space

not zero – tender absence
not zero – face-to-face

Rhyme nor Reason

Surge and silence.
Highminded violence blind-eyes the domiciled,
downplays the wake.

Through the smoke not a vote, a boycott.
In the burning dovecot a well-armed child,
a patriotic snake.

Government cars protect the stars, queue for Victim Assistance.
The Commander-in-Chief enlists belief, 'Call me
Head of Resistance.'

Patrol, rattle and shake. Tacticians on the take.
Told-you shows, faith insistence.
Re-run news, the fight to choose a branded education.
Parents shout their pumped-up doubts, infants
learn an occupation.

It's drought on drought for those without,
greed succeeds in oasis reservations.
Gold dust clogs the lake.

★

'LAW not AWE' you'd painted, on a house-sale board,
dragged it with care to Trafalgar Square
        with friends from 'the horde'.
You said that, still, all comes to nil
before unholy power.

A year later, a week I'd wager, maybe just an hour,
you saw the door a second for sure and slipped right through it,
martyr mentor on the make.

★

You select young men – 'for the cause'.
They hate themselves but crave applause.
You keep them childish, cloddish, loud.
They can arrange a crowd.

Martial measures are a sacred pleasure:
they'd love to lift a trigger finger,
participate in putsch, paramilitary law.
They give thanks for your earnest angst –
                    they've rage in store –

and you feed the need, their urge,
that half-lurk, half-linger
in their hexistential ache.

You persuaded me – once upon a jangling dirge –
but then I fell awake.

★

Your 'Holy' specialises in Told-you-so,
hogs home and hope.

Have faith in what we can know,
widen your scope.

★

My rhythm and rhyme change all the time –
you'd like to help, if I only knew it.
And my views – they're just as loose. Why
                    do I overdo it?
Tics and tricks are tough to take.

Those last words I thought I heard – at least
                    that's how I construe it –
leap up now, or, no, I won't pursue it.

★

Victory! (evisceration)

Victory! (evacuation)

Victory! –

its bomb-like exclamation.

★

We were wise to wash advice
right down, with a drink to ideas.
I don't offer youth or years for denial.
We'd almost be lovers, near sisters, near brothers,
if your conscience hadn't launched its show retrial.

You're too clever for forever cults.
You always knew the mode to mock,
how spiritual leaders force-feed us for air-to-ground results,
under what pressure a fissure starts in rock,
when fondness fails, when competing hearts crack, break.

It's just... what we discussed? years before? –

For goodness sake.

No, wrong crowd. Poor light.

My mistake.

The Line

Countless

Countless, or you could
count away the crowds,
look openly, all
the faces, soft

and some will not soften.
(Not, no. My silence.)

Who are you

glimpsing, gazing,
counting in, up, out,

counting on
the countless?

Informer

In to PROTESTERS
the of phone their formed
shield workmen up

The complained
10-metre-high
from to four to Now

taken strong-arm repel
were call back-up
last-ditch stop

going
Campaigner said
going them are

been since Wednesday
will move go
workmen 9am

the returning officers
station later
is a because is is

around have the deal
and advise council
to out the the

by themselves

have the on
to work completed
the I and workmen

was sit hole
began they
it's but have

to to
bits time won't
with will all

have passed by who
by discontinue
and area obviously

we but
not comment
had off support

including He
can't it approached
Informer

Informer

employee £10,500
on for an employee
inside mastermind

armed been three
behind the raid
three

teenage accomplices
Court and bound
the Burger

him
He told
had with at

away the meticulously
to of friends
Fairmead

14-year-old be legal
the October
he alone

as cashing
balaclava-clad
the with driver

off takings
bags an the closed
heard idea

raid and after
talked
members group believed

planned crime information
the searched
recovering the

an and on
a and
order

who 13
time raid
to He

robbery found
a this
said had

crime terms
had expected
through He

initial were make-believe
maybe all the
the These

take a
and Sentencing
Judge said

a
at leaving victim
while

£10,477.13

custodial suffice
as to
Informer

Informer

Kids risk manhole mothers
risking playing
pot-hole say

The complaints about wide
an at of
on Farm Way

House children and are on
She small been quite
done them kids

here racing riding
and only if there
bad top the

so even can up be it
dangerous be to lid
down You

children because to eye they
Margaret four on said
that have open is
They
but kid down their easily
son already ankle

of holes Everyone
the we football green
you could ankle Worse

A Richmond explained
holes manhole for
and accept a said

have the nobody it
We with now has
to He pledged

the by of
Mrs I to
because it taken

fall hole
hurt
before

have Mrs I
doubt would done
the get

Informer

The line

Let me first our thoughts
our thoughts at this difficult
at this difficult our thoughts
are on thoughts
are in
this difficult
difficult the thoughts
this difficult family

and a deliberate
this deliberate
act of act of
deliberate acting
this deliberate acting
acting act of
this deliberate act of apology.

Our our is with the us of our our
immediate medium term internal
immediate internal
public private
full public a terrible
full us at this hour
full private medium a cool
a cool hard
this organisation this accident
no place
hardly a
place in this hardly
a place in this
unreservedly no place
suspended unreservedly the no.

And advice
advice on the advice
advice of the us
advice from the us
advice for the us
a word to the
to the
a word to the advice
advice from our
our advice
on the advice
on the advice of our
vice of our
on the advice of our
ad
on the advice of senior
senior
on senior the of
on the advice of of
on the of of of
on the advice
on the advice of our
advice of our
advice of our the
on the advice of our line

Griefy train

HIGH QUAL1TY BRANDED WATCHES FROM $150 carefully

address used to words shining bridge. bread
favour servants explain. but anything wonderful
and however. taken course truth free human, next
occasion winter cold use, either tears day
garden. as meant justice dare a. seven pleasure
important? love mist buy yours bear ground.

The snow gets it

The snow gets it, last place to go.
Colour on it, just so you know.

Nothing doing, reflection all.
Something owing, light to crawl.

End of the earth, beginning the same.
Always a – , never a name.

The snow gets it, last place to go.
Colour on it, just so you know.

Waymoat

as a ramping down awareness preveillance
perimeter rejuvenation

releasing the recovery vocal in the selfroad ringhelp
ethical flyunder shine

neighbourhide wash beacon affiliate
daily and natural

gerunds going urgency polish drift
gloating forward

dust balance not in our front end extraface
shore loan

literary fiery charred shoulder
fatnotes

cognition key on the presager-side
median penalty loss enhancer

retail hazard bypass
heavy applicant crossing

compulsory selfpossession ardour

    serried punks

fast decelerating in the rear vie admirer

    art-based textist

give way to coming-on terrific

    collagen lamps

previous turnoff graphic-calming workplan

    outscreech

jack-wifed on the sensual reservation

    stay with the car, stay with the car

wind-drag co-deficient team-colours ratio

    slaproad

child-lock inertia seatbelts in time of were

    armoured nostalgia scold run

plasma scanned reserve tank

    baby in boot

beep –
beep – if you're ambivalent

Ties

In wardrobes, ties hang like curing fish, patterns like smoke. (In restaurants, avoid kippers and sauce.) 'She said she wasn't ready to be tied down. I was gutted.'

It's the tries that bind. In class, at an interview, at weddings. All those boys getting hurt under their collars. Man, it's their funeral.

Ties are universal: presenters of International Poverty Specials receive faxes about their ties. Spokesmen, always getting themselves in knots.

Bosses have a million hang-ups, but they keep you in suspense. They say: 'Don't get shirty with me!'

Fractal teardrops are called 'Paisley pattern', but they happen to be Indian. They're diamonds, stretching a point – to the end of the Silk Road.

A moth started all this, a moth will finish it.

Darkness and Dazzle

after Cavalcanti

Question time

The lady did ask, so here's my answer:
it's an accident. It's arrogant, it's severe,
maybe it's from above. They call it love.
I'll start the task, but please, the chancer,
the bully, best be absent. The accent here
is surely not on shove. They call it love.

This is theoretical science,
not duty or compliance, not plodding measure.
And who has the leisure for the fantastic?
This is the nature of it all, the ecstatic,
the energy defining love's defiance.
Forget beauty or mythical quest: our reliance must rest on that
                                                        treasure
that's composed of atoms, on knowing pleasure through physicist
                                                        tactic,
not romance, not the Church, not the vacuous vatic.

Love starts life where memory is already living.
It makes the most of its generous host: strikes it dead.
Love is formed, if I'm right, as clarity is formed by light –
by darkness, strife. Love's the opposite of giving.
Its name's a boast, its baby-clothes religious robes, red
for Mars, for fevered blight, for the more than war of its constant
                                                        fight.

Love derives from vision, I mean optics, sight,
yet distorts the light reflected from what it sees.
Intelligence, it decrees, must be taken – and taken by force.
It's soon hurt, of course:
it's in foreign territory, powerless, panicked (eventually, every
                                                conqueror's plight).
For intelligence, delight and love's lethal look-at-me's
are neither here nor there. Intelligence just searches, thinks. It can't
                                                        endorse
an image. It lets love depict the damage, howl itself hoarse.

Love, in reality, is not one of the senses –
it's an appetite (I'm here to cite the current thinking).
Besotted with the now-or-never, it's neither cute nor clever,
it separates salvation from sanity with refracting lenses,
calls open season on frivolous reason without the effort of blinking.
Vice is its 'bestest friend forever and ever'.

Love's power can overpower itself, flail out of hand,
but in the end it still can't stand in reason's way. Nothing's that
                                                        strong.
Love isn't wrong, exactly, or against the natural order.
It's just misdirected, distracted, beyond its rightful border –
but everyone here will understand
you're unwomanned, you're unmanned, if you're out of control
                                                        for long
(and you're dead if you disobey love, if you can't applaud her).

Love's way of life is desire,
desire so strong it's beyond right and wrong, all measure.
Love can't fall asleep. At least, not that deep –
it has to be up, creating strife, harsh, abrupt, stoking its secret fire.
All along – mouthing its knowing song, crying, mocking pleasure –
love compels the loved to creep, retreat, contemplate the leap.

Well, it doesn't last,
and no one human is aghast at love's brash actions.
The sighful dissatisfactions are known, too, to almost all –
the fierce gaze, the flat daze, the unreciprocating wall.
Mere anger is surpassed
by love's vast rage, the range of its wrath. Yet love's reactions
paralyse itself, full stop, at point of attraction; self-appal.
And then: nothing at all. Love can't run for fumble or fun with any
                                                        other –
                    it can't walk, it can't crawl.

From a corresponding sensibility, though,
love can attract the moment's fact of a glance.
If it's real to the eyes, love won't jeopardise
the opportunity. Beauty, finally there for love, appears to love so
                                        gentle, so tender.
                                                It's so
lethal. Love's attacked at the giving act of beauty's award dinner
                                                dance.
Pierced by the prize, longing, yearning, subsides. Love falters, falls,
                                                dies.

No, you can't understand love by just having a look.
Understand spotless white, say – write that in your book – but
                                don't think you can
                                        comprehend
this little topic. (We're coming to lecture's end.) Listen closely –
                                abstract, essential,
                                        form
can't be seen, even less its radiation. Its norm

is invisibility. Love is set in darkness – it's been shook
from ordinary life, grammar, duty (a crook would tell you
                                different, pretend
passion's without end – half sweetness, half light). No, love is night
                                of night, dark
                                matter, torn
and tearing, anti-giving, anti-right – but I would say to the lady, I
                                would say to the
                                        lady,
from love, mercy is born.

Well, you can leave safely now, speech, song,
and go where you like. I'd be surprised,
once analysed, if a bard's award wasn't yours, a verse-celeb sinecure, a prof's shiny
                                        gong.
And if I'm wrong – if I'm wrong – this exclusive throng will still position pure
                                        cognition
                                above what sells.
Lady, I have no passion for anyone else.

Darkness and dazzle

Ask, answer.
Accident, arrogant. Call it love.

Deny it, expertise.
Cynics, please, and crude.
Refined science,
not forensics.

This is energy, ecstasy,
love, love –
oh and signs.

Love starts,
obliterates. Love is
darkness,
darkness.

Love senses, sees.
Intelligence by force, as if.
Astonished in foreign territory.

Intelligence shines,
perpetual searchlight.
Considers,
can't make up.

Love's appetite,
current.
Sanity and salvation separate,
intention replaces reason:
vice loves best.

Power – often suicidal,
long
against nature –
distracted,
forget you're alive
(you're dead if you forget).

Love's desire,
beyond measure of nature,
can't sleep.
Rearranging
colours, turning one laugh unstoppable,
affection scared into shadow.

Well.
All agree who suffer it.
Grip commands
a gaze, one miragey place.
An anger, a blazing.
Look.
Attracted? Paralysed.
Anywhere else.
From a
glance, though, though, though,
pleasure.

That replying glimpse,
and yet lethal,
yearning's reality,
sharp-pointed prize.

No, don't think
I don't think.
Listen closely –
it's radiation.

Set in darkness –
no fraud, someone to trust –
dark matter, birth, mercy.

Rotavator

Non-reflective glass

I'd lost a ringpull she gave me,
both slaughtered on a glorified traffic island.
There'd been an impromptu engagement –
29th of March but 'still a leap year – answer yes or no'.
I was in a hurry, I'd cut my knuckle on the metal.
'Uh-huh but you'd need to sign a pre-nuptial.'
I dripped blood on her elasticated cuff
but she wouldn't sign my office trousers.
She said she was against self-harm –
personally, she preferred a more... distributive philosophy –
she might not marry me now.
'It's not all about you, you know –
could we have a trial,
a trial relationship?'

I lost a drawing she gave me.
Her step-nephew had crayoned a five-piece sequence,
crocuses I think, yellow over the lines,
and red plus blue is how you make purple, conceptually speaking.
He was in his final year at the Royal College of Art,
or it might have been Sandhurst,
and she'd helped him with his maths, with his Bible references.

She lost track of me. There had been a year of letters.
She'd wanted to travel to all the territories with spring flowers on
their stamps,
mail me with her travelogues.
They were personal, holy, she cautioned,
but could I 'publish them up' as widely as possible,
have them digitised for a gallery? She'd let me write the preface, or sing.

She'd journeyed first to the Summer Isles but the issuing office had
long since closed,
'This damned archipelago is all seals and scenery.'
Belgium's black flowers looked sinister but it might have been ironic,
"Art's more important if it's tackling the issues, yeah?"
No news for weeks and then Madagascar. 'They respect their
ancestors here,

by the by. Why did you never respect my ancestors?
Dig the bones out and so on.
All I ever wanted you to do
was *respect my ancestors.*'

Colour is seldom so close
but the crocus photographs she despatched
(why no stamps this time? –
that was a wet walk to the depot
and I was distracted; I didn't appreciate having to bluff my ID) –
but the crocus photographs she despatched from who knows where
could be 'blooming planets circling up'.
So Ruth-my-sister's-daughter says
(not Stella's Ruth, obviously, is what I'm saying – 'my' Ruth)
and maybe Filmic is right – just eight and some critic –
they weren't flowers at all
but entities somewhere near the improvised edge of the universe,
vast agglomerations of minerals hurtling towards us
made still, made delicate, by distance.

You can't talk cogently through photography,
focus blurs thought,
but I've set her images beneath non-reflective glass,
a gallery in the hall,
and we could talk colour theory, neuroscience, astronomy
at her own private view if she'd just RSVP
or, at least, send some scribble of a crocus,
proof that she has survived another winter
that a certain armour plated flower has pierced one more enamelled
                                                                                           frost.

Like a student gardener

Like a student gardener at the renovated mansion, sawing old
                                        Beetles in half
and restoring them in compact
compressions, the hangar galvanised by music,
I'd liked, more than liked – 'befonded' she said –
a student gardener at the state-rescued mansion, hearing old Beatles
                                        tunes as half
transferrals from her compact
disc (her on-off vocals supplied all the music).

A lock had been broken. The student gardener at the National
                                        Trust mansion
had destroyed a whole room of beetles – half
a tray, too, of moths, half butterflies, some specimens in compact
glass cases, some simply pins and black spots on cartridge paper,
                                        like written music.

Then – no student, no gardener. At the hydropathic mansion a
                                        doctor beetles and half
confesses to a black magic compact
forced on the best labourers with simplistic operatic music.
One look from that student gardener and the whole remodelled
                                        mansion
would have crashed its crenellations, become King of the Belittleds,
deverticaled to less than its half.

Just one look – beyond videocom, pact,
beyond secret understanding. Well, her glance – your glance –
was always renaissance music –

a master gardener renovating the common parklands, seeing
                                        sparrows, stag beetles return
                                        and half
singing, half humming, believing this compact
rolling ball – they call it the world – could be restored, maybe
                                        maybe maybe,
(the neuro-plasticity of the Earth) with fragile, self-forgetting music.

Golden Key

A person reading –
truth and tree share the same root.

A woman reading –
singing – it's you, singing
(under your breath).

> *Golden key, golden key.*
> *Let yourself in,*
> *let yourself in –*
> *you can*
> *let yourself in*
> *with this golden key.*

You're reading – it's a simulation
of a book –
book and bark share the same root.

Light coming up, a little audio.
The Ancient Forest? New Songs? The Spiral Tower?

> *Golden key, golden key.*
> *Let yourself in.*